MADE BY

THY

The Proof In The Flash

DR. ABRAHAM KHOUREIS, Ph.D.

Copyright Notice

Table of Contents

Introduction 1

Chapter 1: The Proof in the Flesh................................3

Chapter 2: The First Touch of Life..............................7

Chapter 3: The Human Finger 11

Chapter 4: A Pattern That Outlives Time 15

Chapter 5: The Observation 19

Chapter 6: The Print That Cannot Lie 23

Chapter 7: No Two Fingerprints Alike........................27

Chapter 8: The Signature That Speaks Without Ink ...31

Chapter 9: Ten Fingers, One Identity 35

Chapter 10: Fingerprint of The Divine 39

Chapter 11: The Invention of the Print 43

Chapter 12: When the Law Looks for Proof, It Turns to the...

Finger 47

Chapter 13: The Maker Is Not Silent...........................51

Chapter 14: Designed, Not Necessary 53

Chapter 15: The Question of Proof 57

Chapter 16: Each Finger Speaks a Purpose 61

Chapter 17: Our Fingerprint Has Memory...................65

Chapter 18: When Identity Fails, the Fingerprint Remains..69

Chapter 19: The First Impression Is Lasting 73

Chapter 20: The Final Proof, Touched, Signed, Sent..........76

Chapter 21: The Signature We Never Asked For................79

Chapter 22: The Hand of the Maker.............................83

Chapter 23: When the Finger Touches the World............87

Chapter 24: When the Finger Is Gone 90

Chapter 25: The Invisible Ink 93

Chapter 26: The Twin That Never Was........................97

Chapter 27: The Reflection of the Maker 99
Chapter 28: When Data Points to Design 103
Chapter 29: Made by Thy 105
Chapter 30: You Are Free to Disagree.............................109
Chapter 31: Author's Final Notes....................................113
Interview with the Author – "Q&A".................................117
References – Recommended Readings 123
About Dr. Abraham Khoureis, Ph.D................................125
Other Books by Dr. Abraham 127

"Your fingerprint is the first biography written about you, long before your name was given."

Dr. Abraham Khoureis

This page intentionally left blank for your reading reflection

Introduction

This is not a religious book. Nor is it merely spiritual. It may touch science, it may evoke faith, but above all, it is a reflection on something real. Something you carry.

Something I have seen with my own eyes thousands of times. One of the companies I own and manage in Los Angeles, California, is a background screening company, where part of my office work involved fingerprinting clients. For over 15 years, and to the present, day after day, human after human, they came, different in every possible way. Different races. Different ages. Different belief systems. Men, women, and those who do not identify with either. People born in different lands, speaking different languages and dialects, but every single one of them carried something no one else ever had: A fingerprint that was theirs alone. I do not mean similar. I mean never repeated.

I began noticing patterns. Not just the ridges and whorls under the lens, but something deeper: a message, perhaps even a signature. Over time, as I examined thousands of fingerprints, I became overwhelmed by a quiet realization, this is not random. This is not chance. This is not some fluke of biology.

This is a signature mark. Perhaps, a divine one.

No two humans have the same fingerprint. Not even twins. Not even clones. And while we all share similar organs, similar capacities, and yes, even similar stories, the Maker of this Being saw fit to give each of us one physical trait that could never be duplicated: the fingerprint.

That is where the idea for this book was born.

What began as a professional task slowly turned into a spiritual awakening, a scientific curiosity, and a deep human observation. The fingerprint is not just a way to verify who we are. It is a subtle declaration that we are made. Intentionally. Uniquely. Purposefully.

This book is my attempt to follow that trail. To ask why. To explore what this mark might mean, not just for our identity, but for our existence. If you are holding this book, you too have that mark. You, too, are proof. The manifestation is the human being. And the fingerprint?

It is the quiet signature and mark of Thy.

Chapter 1
The Proof in the Flesh

It began, not with a vision, or a revelation, but with a fingerprint scan. For over 15 years, one of the companies I have owned and operated is a background screening company in Los Angeles, California. Day in, day out, people came from all walks of life: teachers, doctors, attorneys, caregivers, nurses, janitors, actors, immigrants, and executives, to name few. They placed their fingers on a DOJ/FBI certified scanner, and for a few moments, their print became data.

As an MIT Machine Learning Data Science Advanced Program graduate through Great Learning, I learned to turn data into insights. What struck me wasn't the name, the profile, or the purpose of the screening. What struck me, over, and over, was how each print was entirely its own. Some were curved like quiet rivers. Some arched like rising waves. Some twisted in whorls that looked almost too perfect to have grown from skin.

No two fingerprints alike. Not once. Not even close.

In my MBA organizational behaviors classes, my students and I talk about human uniqueness, about different personalities, what motivates others, and cultivates the self; and with my SAG-AFTRA represented talent, we talk about imitating or mimicking voices, and Hollywood shared dreams. But human fingerprints... it is the one thing none have shared, even if they share your blood, your birthday, or your story. Your fingerprints are uniquely yours and yours alone. It is proven, permanent, and silent. From infancy to death, it remains unchanged, as if to say: *"This one, this exact one although similar to others in creation, was made only once and the fingerprint is the proof."*

We casually leave our fingerprints on glasses, on door handles, on the windows we press our hands against. Sometimes we wipe them away, embarrassed by the trace. As time passes, I start to believe that each fingerprint is a quiet declaration, not just of identity, but of authorship.

When a painter signs a canvas, he/she leaves his/her name. When a builder brands a brick, they mark their work. And when a Being is made, fashioned, not assembled, there may remain a trace... a fingerprint. A signature of creation, of authorship.

Not ours.

But, of the One who made us.

Scientists tell us fingerprints are formed in the womb, influenced by blood flow, movement, pressure, and timing. I am not writing this book to contradict science.

Nor support religious doctrines, I write this book to ask a question science cannot answer:

Why the need for difference?

If randomness alone shaped us, or made us, surely some fingerprints would repeat. Surely, some cosmic accident would duplicate at least once, just once, across the billions who walk the Earth. But it doesn't happen. The fingerprint remains stubbornly individual. Stubbornly uniquely yours.

So, I ask again: *Why?*

This book is my reflection on that question. It is not a sermon.

Not a doctrine.

But it is an offering, born of awe, written in observation, and carried by something deeper than logic alone.

If my assumption is correct, the proof of creation, if it exists, is not in the sky.

But, it is in your hand.

This page intentionally left blank for your reading reflection

---

Chapter 2

The First Touch of Life

Before our eyes open to the light of this world, something quiet takes place beneath the surface of the skin. Deep within the womb, before we know language, before we know the meaning of pain or hope or belonging, the first lines of identity begin to appear. These thin ridges are formed in a rhythm we cannot witness, but they form nevertheless, in that gentle sanctuary that becomes our first home. The womb teaches us that identity is not delivered to us by society. It is prepared long before society knows our name.

Scientists explain that fingerprint patterns begin forming around the thirteenth week of pregnancy. They emerge as the skin develops from two layers that fold into one another as if following instructions that existed long before our conception.

Even the slightest shift in the amniotic environment influences the pattern. A small movement of the hand, a brief turn of the developing fingers, and the shape takes a new direction. The process does not repeat for any other human. The conditions that shape one print never occur again in the same order. We carry the outcome without

7

ever remembering how it happened.

When I first learned about this biological process, I felt something very human about it. I understood science well enough to respect its structure, but I could not ignore the quiet meaning behind it. The formation of fingerprints is not dramatic. It is not visible. It is not loud. It happens in silence, without applause and without any witness. Yet it creates a signature that lasts a lifetime. Something about that gently reminded me that important things do not always announce themselves. Sometimes they happen in a quiet environment.

For most of my life, like thousands, and I may dare millions, fingerprints were simply a method of identification, a tool used in professional work, something practical and necessary. I used to see them daily, rolled on ink pads, scanned through digital readers, printed and recorded. Yet every time I examined another print, I felt as if I was standing before a snowflake that had never melted. Not once did I hear of an exact fingerprints repetition. Not once did the Designer decide to copy His/her own design. I began to feel that individuality was not a choice. It was a gift we arrived with.

There is something humble about the first weeks of life. We enter existence without choice, yet something in the unseen chooses a pattern for us that does not belong to anyone else. A child does not decide its genetic code. The womb does not allow negotiation. Life begins and the pattern is assigned. Later in life we search for identity in achievements, titles, and recognition, yet the most permanent form of identity was given to us before we knew how to ask for it.

Some people wonder if fingerprints have any deeper purpose. Scientists say their ridges help the skin grip surfaces and sense touch. Others suggest the arrangement improves tactile sensitivity. These explanations are valid, measurable, and meaningful. But there is also a meaning that science does not need to prove. A meaning we sense without relying on evidence. The pattern itself speaks its own language. It tells us that individuality is purposeful.

I have fingerprinted thousands of human beings. Many were people I would never meet again. Some were young, some were old, some were nervous, and some curious.

I remember the quiet moments when someone placed their finger on the scanner. The print appeared instantly on the screen. The person would often lean forward to look at it. They would stare as if seeing something for the first time. In their eyes I would witness a moment of realization. They did not expect their skin to hold so much detail. I could tell that something inside them awakened, even if only for a second.

I often think of the unborn child whose fingers are still forming. That child already carries the print of a destiny that has not yet unfolded. We rarely think of ourselves this

way, yet this is the truth. Our story begins before our consciousness arrives. We arrive holding a message written on us without ink and without words, yet unmistakably our own.

Somewhere in the process of becoming adults we forget this beginning. We forget that life was personal from its first moment. We forget that identity was not assigned by society, but by existence itself. When I think of my own early formation, I feel a quiet gratitude. Something in the universe prepared me before I knew how to prepare myself.

If that is true for me, it is true for every person who has ever lived.

This first touch of life does not belong to religion or science alone. It belongs to the human being who carries it. It belongs to the person who wakes every morning unaware that the most permanent truth about them rests on their own fingertips.

And so, before we search for meaning in complicated places, perhaps it is worth remembering that our identity was created in silence. It began with a touch inside the womb, long before we learned how to reach for the world.

Chapter 3

The Human Finger

Before we speak of the fingerprint, we must first consider the human finger. Not the metaphorical finger that points to the heavens, nor the accusatory finger we often raise at one another, but the physical finger. This humble extension of the hand, this tool we use daily without reverence, without pause. The finger touches, holds, writes, signs, types, draws, soothes, and points. It is an instrument of both power and tenderness. But even more than that, it is the only part of the human body that carries an unchanging, individualized design visible to the eye.

The finger, in its anatomy, is miraculous enough. Bones, tendons, nerves, vessels, all arranged in such harmony that it can lift a feather or hold a hammer. It can crack an egg, button a shirt, perform surgery, or trigger a weapon. It is a tool of the mind made flesh. But it is what sits atop the skin on the very surface, that most astonishes. A pattern. A swirl. A labyrinth. And that pattern never repeats.

You see, the finger is not just functional. It is an emblem of identity. It touches the world, yes, but it also tells the world, I am here. I am real. I am distinct.

11

In every profession, from hospitals to immigration, from law enforcement to government, from high-security vaults to school enrollment forms, the finger is consulted not for what it can do, but for what it says. And what it says is: No one else is me.

How strange, isn't it? Our face can resemble another's. Our voice can be mimicked. Even our DNA, in rare cases, can be near-identical. But our fingerprint? Impossible to duplicate.

Why?

Why would a biological process, shaped by amniotic pressure, fetal movement, and chance, result in a feature so consistent in its uniqueness?

Why does every finger on every hand across every century bear a different print?

And why, above all, would such a detail exist on a part of us we use to interact with the world?

The ancients once believed that the hand held power. The finger, in particular, was considered divine, used in blessings, in judgments, in oaths.

Today, we use it to unlock our phones.

But perhaps both are right.

We live in a time when humans marvel at the complexity of galaxies and quantum fields. Yet few pause to marvel at the fingertip.

Few look at their hand and ask,

Who designed this? Why this?

In the pages to come, we will explore the print itself, its formation, its scientific relevance, its theological suggestion. But for now, let us rest in the miracle of the finger.

It touches life, but it also speaks life. And the story it tells, quietly, universally, is that every human being is a singular creation. And that is not just a fact. That is what made me wonder.

This page intentionally left blank for your reading reflection

_____

_____

_____

_____

_____

_____

_____

_____

_____

_____

_____

Chapter 4

A Pattern That Outlives Time

There is something quietly powerful about the idea of time. We measure it in years, decades, and generations, yet we forget that our physical presence exists only for a short moment inside a much longer human story. When I started researching for this book, I encountered fingerprint patterns from people who were no longer alive, I realized something extraordinary. Their bodies had disappeared, their voices no longer echoed, their stories might have been forgotten, yet the lines on their fingertips remained visible on paper. The person had passed, but the human mark remained. It was as if time agreed to keep one part of them present.

Fingerprints do not dissolve easily. Police records, immigration documents, notarized files, and identification cards may sit inside archives for decades, even centuries. They survive fires, floods, and transfers from one institution to another. They survive political change, wars, and the disappearance of nations. A print remains as long as the surface that hosts it does not perish. There is something profoundly human about that endurance. It reminds us that life leaves evidence, sometimes in ways we do not notice.

15

When scientists study ancient remains, they often discover preserved fingerprints on pottery, on clay tablets, or on handmade bricks. These prints belonged to people who lived thousands of years ago. They might have built temples, baked bread, constructed walls, or shaped objects for everyday use. Their names faded, their civilizations collapsed, their languages disappeared, yet the physical trace of their touch still exists under microscopes today. I always found this detail striking. Even when memory falls silent, the human mark survives in silence. Hopefully as I write these pages and publish them, in silence no more.

I used to believe that our legacy was entirely based on what we accomplished. We often measure ourselves by achievements, projects, recognitions, and the praise we receive from others. Then I realized something simpler. Our legacy begins much earlier than our accomplishments. It begins the moment our body forms a pattern that no one else will ever carry. That pattern is a summary of identity before identity has even expressed itself through words and actions.

Sometimes we forget how much our existence matters. We grow through hardship, uncertainty, disappointment, and loss. We experience moments when life feels temporary, fragile, or unimportant. Yet our very biology carries a message that contradicts those doubts. The fingerprint says you matter not because of what you do, but because of who you are. It says your existence was intended, not accidental. It says your life carries a pattern that refuses duplication.

I remember a time when the family members of an elderly client came to our office asking for a fingerprint identification card belonging to this individual who had passed away recently. The card reminded me that this person once stood in front of me, once breathed, once laughed, once worried, once dreamed. The ridges on the surface reminded me of their physical presence. They were here. Their body carried a signature that no one else shared. The world may move forward, but the truth of their individuality remains unchanged.

The print revealed nothing about this individual's personality, beliefs, or destiny. It simply confirmed identity. It told me that someone existed with a pattern that could never belong to anyone else. In that moment, the boundaries of time softened. The person lived somewhere in history, but part of them continued in this present moment. Even though our paths will never cross again, our realities touched through those lines imprinted on paper.

It is humbling to realize that our fingerprints outlive us. Not because we have conquered the world, but because creation gave us something permanent. In a way, the fingerprint protects our human story from being erased. Even if people forget our name, even if our achievements are never known, our individuality remains documented somewhere on paper, in a database, or inside a file.

There is a quiet dignity in knowing that time does not fully erase us. Our bodies return to the earth, our voices fall silent, our memories fade in the minds of others, yet something small and unassuming preserves our story. The fingerprint stands like a small monument to our existence.

It reminds me that every human being carries something eternal in their biology. It may not be eternal in the spiritual sense, but it is certainly lasting in the physical world. When we leave this earth, we leave behind a trail that proves we walked here. That, to me, is a powerful truth.

Our existence was recorded biologically, not through opinion or permission. It was embedded in us the moment we formed inside the womb. And that pattern, simple and quiet as it may appear, continues to speak even after we have said our final word.

Chapter 5

The Observation

What I am going to share with you did not begin with a theory.

It began with a scanner.

For over 15 years, I have been in the business of background screening, a job that, on the surface, is simple: verify identity, confirm trustworthiness, capture a set of fingerprints and move on to the next client. The process is fast, procedural, almost forgettable. But over time, something stirred in the background of my noticing.

Thousands passed through my office. Men, women, the elderly, teenagers, teachers, truck drivers, CEOs, caregivers, immigrants, athletes, once even a priest. People from every color and creed. Some joked nervously about their record. Others walked in proud, certain, polished. But regardless of who they were, or why they came, there was one silent moment of truth they all shared. Their fingerprints.

I don't mean their name or their ID; those could be forged. I mean their literal print. Rolled slowly across the scanner glass, revealing whorls, loops, arches, ridges like waves in

19

a sea no one else could replicate. I began to notice: no two ever looked the same. Not even between left and right hands. Not even between thumb and pinky. Even identical twins, who share the same DNA, bore prints that were unmistakably their own.

At first, I dismissed it as biology doing its job. That is what they teach us: fingerprints form in the womb, shaped by movement, pressure, randomness. But what kind of randomness leaves behind a signature? One that never repeats. One that cannot be faked. One so exact that entire legal systems build their trust around it.

The more I observed, the more impossible it became to ignore.

The Why:

Why would the body need this level of uniqueness?

Why would nature insist on variation, not just among us, but within us?

Why would your left index finger not match your right?

Why would every single human, in the billions that have come and gone, be marked with a code that exists nowhere else?

These weren't spiritual questions. Not yet. They were practical, human ones. The kind of questions that creep in when you are alone with data for too long and start to wonder: is this just identity… or something more?

I started to ask people, gently, in conversation, if they ever noticed how distinct their prints were. Most hadn't. They were surprised when I showed them. Some laughed, some paused. A few grew quiet. One man, a former engineer, stared at his fingers for nearly a minute before whispering, "That's… oddly beautiful."

Yes. It was.

This chapter of my life, fingerprint after fingerprint, silent scan after scan, became something else. A meditation. A lesson delivered not in words, but in ridges and spirals. I was no longer just documenting people. I was being shown something through them. Something intricate, unrepeatable, and strangely intimate.

I began to wonder… What if this wasn't just biological utility? What if this was an intentional mark, not just of who we are, but that we are? A reminder left by the One who made us, saying:

"This one is mine. This unique human, I made."

I don't expect everyone to believe that. I am not asking them to. What I offer in this book is not proof, but pattern. A valid observation and a reflection. It began in the quiet rooms of my office, behind glass doors, with the gentle roll of fingertips across a scanner, and a man, a lucky management scholar, and an MIT Machine Learning & Data Scientist (through Great Learning) who started to see more than he was trained for. I offer it now to you, not as certainty, but as a witness.

Chapter 6

The Print That Cannot Lie

It begins before you take your first breath.

In the quiet, dark waters of the womb, while the mother sleeps and cells divide, something remarkable begins to form. Around the sixth week of gestation, your skin starts to take shape. By the tenth to twelfth week, as your tiny fingers press gently against the amniotic sac, an environment so delicate and ever-shifting, the friction between skin, fluid, and pressure begins to carve the most intimate design you will ever carry.

Your fingerprint.

No conscious thought directs this formation. No genetics alone can predict it. In fact, even with identical DNA, as in the case of twins, the fingerprint emerges differently. Why? Because it is not just the genetic code that determines the pattern. It is the microenvironment. The angle of pressure. The slightest variations in uterine wall texture. The subtle movements of the fetal hand. A divine choreography of physics and biology that leaves behind something far greater than the sum of its causes.

By the time you are born, your fingerprint is already

complete. And unless injured deeply, it will remain unchanged for the rest of your life. Through childhood scrapes and adulthood labor, through the softness of age and even into death, the pattern stays. Silent. Loyal. Unforgettable.

But here is where it becomes even more compelling.

Out of the Eight (8) billion humans alive today, not a single one shares your exact fingerprint.

Statistically, the chance of duplication is less than 1 in 64 billion. That means even if the Earth's population doubled, and every person on it had identical twins, your fingerprint would still be yours alone.

This is not poetry. This is science.

Forensic scientists, biometric engineers, and security experts have long relied on this fact. In courts of law, a fingerprint is not just evidence; it is near-certain proof. It is the only human marker, aside from perhaps the iris, that remains virtually impossible to replicate or deny.

Now ask yourself, if this is merely a fluke of biology, why such precision? Why such permanence? Why such uniqueness?

Why would evolution insist on making each human so personally identifiable? Wouldn't general patterns suffice for survival? Wouldn't shared traits be more efficient?

And yet... we are not a copy... we are a unique design.

In ancient scriptures, there are references to the "Book of Life" a record written by God's hand. In science, we speak of the fingerprint as a record written by nature's laws. But perhaps both are reaching for the same truth. Perhaps what we call nature is simply the visible handwriting of the Invisible One.

What if, long before you spoke a word, before you chose a name, before the world could define you, The Maker of this fingerprint had already signed you?

A mark no one could forge. A pattern no one could predict. A print no one could duplicate.

As a professional, certified, and well-trained fingerprint roller, I have fingerprinted thousands of individuals for license and legal purposes. Their eyes told me one story. Their voice another. But it was their finger that always told the truth.

Even when people changed their names, fled from their past, or sought to hide their identity, their fingerprint spoke louder than any lie.

It could not be edited. It could not be denied.

And that is why this chapter bears its title: The Print That Cannot Lie.

It is your original truth.

So let me ask you: what kind of Creator marks every soul with such precision, and then hides that signature in plain sight?

Perhaps,

The One who wants you to find it.

The One who says, "This one... is Mine."

Chapter 7

No Two Fingerprints Alike

There are over eight billion people alive today. And yet, not one fingerprint repeats.

Not one. Strange, isn't it?

Not across the streets of New York or the villages of Ethiopia. Not between a newborn in Seoul or a grandmother in Buenos Aires. Not even among siblings, or twins, or the same person's own left and right hand. The ridges might resemble one another, but they are never identical. Always distinct. Always yours.

Please, please, PAUSE and consider what that means.

In a world that duplicates everything, from cloned plants to copied voices to endless digital replicas, the human fingerprint remains stubbornly, quietly original.

Even the most advanced AI can replicate a style of writing, a face, a voice. But it cannot make a fingerprint that passes as real, not consistently, and not convincingly. Because a fingerprint is not just a pattern. It is an imprint made by pressure, motion, tension, fluid, time, and perhaps something else.

We live in a society that teaches us to look for what is

shared: common ancestors, shared traits, generational patterns. But the fingerprint doesn't follow that path. It doesn't conform. It declares uniqueness, again, and again, and again.

I have held the hands of thousands of people, not in affection, but in protocol. Even in the most ordinary of circumstances, the moment felt sacred. I would guide their thumb gently to the scanner, and for a split second, I would see what no one else ever had: the untouched singularity of that human being.

I never saw the same print twice.

Statisticians and forensic scientists confirm it, even with billions of humans, and billions more who came before us, the chance of identical prints is practically zero. You are not just rare. You are exclusive.

Why?

Why would the universe go to such trouble to ensure you are unlike anyone else?

Science can trace the mechanics, the skin folds in the womb, the random pressure on developing fingers, the way amniotic fluid swirls. But science does not tell us why uniqueness matters. It tells us how, but not why.

If our bodies were built only for survival, sameness would be more efficient. Interchangeable parts, like machines.

But we are not machines. We are not even copies of ourselves.

Your right ring finger doesn't match your left. You carry ten different prints on ten fingers. A personal symphony of ridges and arches, declaring like our own self:

"I am many, and still one."

The more I observed, the more I understood that uniqueness was not a defect. It was design. A signature. A declaration of authorship.

What do you call a signature that cannot be forged, duplicated, or erased?

I call it divine. What do you call it?

But even if you don't, even if you believe in chance, chaos, or cosmic mathematics, you must admit: this level of unrepeatable detail in billions of lives... it is remarkable.

It is not proof. It is not a doctrine. But it is a door.

And once you see it, really see it, you cannot unsee it.

Each person who sits before me, each palm placed on the scanner, each fingertip rolled carefully in ink or light, they all carry a message I did not write but cannot ignore: No two alike. No one forgotten. No being accidental.

This page intentionally left blank for your reading reflection

_____

_____

_____

_____

_____

_____

_____

_____

_____

_____

_____

Chapter 8

The Signature That Speaks Without Ink

A signature is usually written by hand. It is a mark of authorship, a personal stamp that confirms,

I was here. I made this. I accept responsibility.

In courts, contracts, and declarations, a signature is more than a name, it is a binding act. But what if the most important signature you carry... was never written or signed by you?

What if it was never written with ink?

Look at your fingertip. Really look. You will see lines, ridges and valleys forming circles, loops, or arches. You may have memorized their use for unlocking your phone or passing a background check, but you may never have realized you are looking at a signature.

Not yours. But,

Your Maker.

It is the only part of your body where you carry undeniable proof that you were authored, you were made, you were created.

No ink. No pen. No stylus. Every groove is etched with permanence. It cannot be altered without damage. It cannot be replaced. It cannot be forged.

Just as a painter signs a canvas once the masterpiece is complete, the Creator marked His creation, not on the back, not on the inside, but on the very tip of your fingers.

And He didn't just sign one. He signed all ten.

Why?

Because you were meant to know.

You were meant to see it every time you reached, held, touched, or created.

You were meant to carry the signature in your labor, in your art, in your prayer, in your protection of others, and in your own becoming.

This signature speaks to everyone who is willing to look. And the language it speaks is not written in syllables or sounds, but in design.

The fingerprint is not necessary for survival. It is not essential to breathe, to eat, to walk, or to reproduce. Its only purpose, from a strictly biological perspective, is to aid in grip. But does that justify the endless variety?

Does it explain the mathematical impossibility of duplication?

No.

What it does suggest, however, is intent. It indicates something science cannot fully grasp:

This is not randomness.

This is authorship. This is order. And with every order, there is a design, and with every design, there is a designer.

We do not marvel when books have different covers. We marvel when we realize the author wrote each word. Crafted each page. Chose each sentence.

Well, my dear you, you are not just a book.

You are a signed first and only unique edition.

And this signature cannot be erased.

In all my years, I have never seen two prints alike. Not

even close. I have fingerprinted mothers and daughters, fathers and sons, twins, lovers and strangers. But when their finger touched the scanner, it told a different story, I am not her. I am not him. I am me.

Because I know and believe in the conviction that our fingerprints are the Signature and Mark of our Creator, every time I saw it, I felt like I was touching something sacred.

No matter what someone believed, what they did, what they ran from, their fingerprint was honest. And honest things… are holy.

Sometimes, when I felt my significant other stretched the truth, I teased her by telling her I wish you were as honest as your fingerprints. She laughed, and replied, "well, I am as honest as your fingerprints," to a reciprocated tender smile.

Our fingerprint is the only part of our identity the world cannot alter, and the only proof, perhaps, that we were never a coincidence.

We were designed. And we were signed.

Chapter 9

Ten Fingers, One Identity

We often speak of identity as if it is singular. One name. One ID. One self.

But the human body doesn't follow that simplicity. It carries ten different fingerprints on ten fingers, not duplicate images, not variants of the same print, but wholly unique impressions, each formed in the womb through movement, position, and pressure.

And yet, all ten belong to one person.

That paradox, of multiplicity and unity, fascinated me.

I began to ask: why would a single being be marked ten different times? Why wouldn't our fingers carry one shared signature, like a seal stamped ten times over? Wouldn't that be more efficient, more consistent?

But that is not how we were made.

Each finger testifies: you are not merely one thing. You are a composite. A gathering. A mystery housed in skin and bone and breath.

And still… you are you.

Ten distinct prints, and yet they lead back to the same person. In a forensic lab, all ten fingers point to one identity. One self, expressed ten ways.

It reminds me of how we live.

We are not the same version of ourselves everywhere. We are different with a child than we are with a colleague. We are different when grieving than when celebrating. Different in solitude than in conversation. But the core remains. The one who feels it all. The one who carries it.

This is more than metaphor. It is design.

Your hands, your very fingers, declare it.

The thumb, strong, steady, opposable.

The index, the finger of command and direction.

The middle, longest, often most visible, most often misunderstood.

The ring, for union, for tradition, for promises.

The pinky, small, but no less essential to grip and balance.

Each finger plays its role. Each print plays its part.

No two are alike, but all belong to the same being.

Is it possible, then, that the Designer, whoever or whatever brought us into being, left us this quiet architecture as a reminder?

That our identity is not flattened to one trait, one label, one act? That we are meant to be multifaceted, and still, at our center, whole?

When staff at my office welcomes my clients and roll each of their ten fingers onto a scanner, we don't just see prints anymore. We see a kind of silent poetry: ten expressions, one author.

It reminds me that our identity like the human Self is never fixed and singular. It is layered. Lived. Evolving. Rotating, and still, unmistakably ours.

No machine could invent such subtlety.

Ten fingers. Ten testimonies. One self.

And maybe, just maybe, a quiet reminder of the Maker who knew that being human would require more than one way to touch the world.

"Does man think that We will not assemble his bones? Nay, We are able to put together in perfect order the very tips of his fingers."

(Holy Qur'an 75:3–4)

Chapter 10

Fingerprint of The Divine

Across history, whenever the Divine made contact with humanity, it was rarely subtle. Seas parted. Fire descended. Words were etched into stone. But perhaps the most powerful moment, one that unites faiths, legends, and truths, is when it is said that God Himself wrote with His finger.

In the Book of Exodus, we are told that the Ten Commandments were written "by the finger of God." These were not just laws. They were divine declarations, carved not by the hand of a prophet, but by the Creator Himself. Stone tablets turned sacred not merely because of their message, but because of who inscribed them.

Why does that matter here?

Because the belief is that the same God who once inscribed stone... has inscribed you.

Not on a tablet. Not on parchment. But on flesh.

Your fingerprint is not just your identity; it is His Signature.

When we imagine God's finger, we often picture it

reaching toward man, as in Michelangelo's fresco. A moment of touch, spark, and breath. But what if we have misunderstood that scene? What if God didn't just touch man once? What if He continues to touch every human being, not with lightning or voice, but with His quiet, unmistakable mark?

We see this idea repeated in every tradition:

In **Judaism**, God is the One who "knits us together in the womb."

In **Christianity**, the Holy Spirit descends upon each soul as uniquely as fingerprints differ.

In **Islam**, long before science recognized the uniqueness of fingerprints, the Qur'an 1415 centuries ago pointed to the fingertips as evidence of human individuality and divine knowledge of the human form.

God says, **"Does man think We will not assemble his bones? Nay, We are able to put together his fingertips with perfect precision."** (Quran, Surah Al-Qiyamah, 75:3-4).

Why fingertips?

Of all the body's parts, why would a sacred text thousands of years old highlight fingertips?

Science didn't know in the 7th century that fingerprints were unique. There were no scanners, no ink pads. Here it is, a divine claim of perfect reconstruction down to the individualized part of you.

That verse does not merely suggest resurrection. It declares authorship. You were written. You were authored. You were created. And like any great work, the author leaves behind something unmistakable. A signature.

I remember once fingerprinting a man, tough exterior, quiet demeanor, no particular interest in anything beyond the task. As his print appeared on the screen, he stared at it silently. After a moment, he asked, "So... no one else in the world has this?"

"No one," I said.

He paused. Then said, "That's... kinda wild."

I smiled, at the time, he didn't know he was having a spiritual moment. But he was.

Because once you realize that your fingertip is an unrepeatable inscription, not chosen by you, not even fully explained by science, you are left with one possibility: Someone signed you.

Our Maker didn't just write you once. He wrote you into being. He wrote you as proof. You are not a vessel of random dust.

We are the living parchment of our Maker's Touch.

This page intentionally left blank for your reading reflection

_____

_____

_____

_____

_____

_____

_____

_____

_____

_____

_____

Chapter 11

The Invention of the Print

No two alike. Ten per person. Eight billion walking examples. And yet... we rarely stop to ask why.

Why fingerprints? Why this complex pattern on such a small surface? Why not a smoother skin, or a less elaborate design? Why were we made this way?

Science tells us that the purpose of fingerprints is grip. The ridges, or friction ridges, increase our ability to hold onto surfaces. That may be true. And it may be useful. But if utility were the only objective, then nature could have opted for a far simpler form, one repeated across all fingers, or one borrowed from animals who grip better than us.

Instead, nature, or what I call the Designer, chose complexity. It chose difference. It invented the print. And not just the idea of the fingerprint as a physical marker, but the fingerprint as an identity code. An imprint so personalized, so precise, that it can identify someone decades later, long after memory fades, voices change, and photos decay.

It makes you wonder... Who was this invention for?

A baby in utero will begin forming fingerprints by the 10th week. By the time they're born, the unique ridge patterns are set and will remain unchanged throughout life. Even as the body grows, shrinks, scars, or ages, the print holds.

Nothing we wear or learn or inherit stays with us that consistently.

Not our hair. Not our beliefs. Not even our name.

But our fingerprint remains.

So, I ask again: Why?

Why would a print be written onto us before we ever speak a word?

Some say it is evolution. Others call it randomness. But I have spent years scanning and observing these patterns, day after day, client after client. And I can tell you, randomness doesn't leave this kind of signature.

Randomness does not replicate meaning so consistently across the human species, with zero repetition.

There is order here. Not chaos. Precision. Not accident.

To invent the fingerprint is not just to label a person, it is to tell the world: "This one is not like the others."

It is to embed that truth into the flesh.

This is no different than a sculptor leaving a hidden mark beneath the stone. Or a painter embedding initials into a corner of the canvas. Not for the public to notice, necessarily. But for the Artist to say,

"This one came from my hand."

You might say I'm romanticizing the body.

Perhaps I am. But I am doing it with my eyes open.

When you have rolled as many prints as I have, when you have held as many hands, seen as many ridges, observed as many quiet spirals of skin, the question no longer becomes

"Do I believe in a Designer and a Creator?"

The question becomes,

"How could I not?"

Each human being, stamped at formation, marked without their permission, with a print that gently and silently reminds us: We were made.

That, to me, is the invention of the print. Not a function. Not a fluke. But a sign and a logical reminder that every design requires the presence of a Designer. And every creation requires the existence of a Creator.

This page intentionally left blank for your reading reflection

---

Chapter 12

When the Law Looks for Proof, It Turns to the Finger

In a courtroom, truth is everything.

We rely on evidence to speak when memory fails. We call on documentation, records, and witnesses to verify what happened, who was there, and what was said. But among all forms of evidence, few carry the weight, certainty, and finality of a fingerprint.

When the law wants the truth, it turns to the finger.

You can lie with words. You can alter a document. You can disguise your face, change your name, flee to another land. But one thing always remains unchanged, unforgeable, and unrepeatable: your fingerprint.

Governments across the globe have built entire systems on this truth. From national ID cards to criminal databases, from immigration checkpoints to birth records, the fingerprint has become a universal signature of identity.

And still, most people do not ask why.

Why did the Creator design a mark so distinct, so exact, so enduring, that it would become the ultimate proof of who we are?

If identity were meant to be fluid, why root it so firmly in flesh?

If we were nothing but evolved matter, why give us a feature no other creature has in such complexity?

Only humans bear this kind of print.

Apes have ridges. So do koalas. But they do not have our level of detail, variability, and permanence. The human fingerprint stands apart, a conscious stamp on the canvas of skin. And for over a century, forensic science has trusted it as the most reliable form of physical evidence.

Why would the courts, with all their logic and skepticism, rely so deeply on this simple mark?

Because deep down, we all know: this doesn't lie.

In my line of work, I have seen what fingerprints uncover. I have witnessed people try to hide from their past, changed appearances, new identities, and yet one scan of their finger brought the truth forward.

In less than a second, who they were confronted who they claimed to be.

Not out of vengeance. Not out of cruelty.

But because the fingerprint knows.

It doesn't age. It doesn't forget. It doesn't care about your story, it is your story.

It is the only part of your physical body that says: This is me. This has always been me. This will always be me.

So, the law turns to it. The system relies on it. And the world agrees: the fingerprint is the ultimate witness.

But what of the One who designed it?

If human courts believe this mark is sufficient for judgment, might not divine courts as well?

It is not far-fetched to imagine that, one day, when all masks are removed, and the soul stands bare, God will not need to ask your name. He will only need to look at your hand.

And He will say, "I know you. I signed you Myself."

The irony is that most people live their whole lives

carrying this proof, using it daily, placing it on forms, doors, screens, and glass, yet never realizing what it truly is.

A witness. A proof. A mark of origin.

And the law, in its pursuit of truth, unknowingly bows to the fingerprint, not as a random feature of biology, but as the evidence that something greater made this human.

When man wants the truth and wants you found, he looks to the finger.

Perhaps, so does the Creator.

Chapter 13

The Maker Is Not Silent

If the fingerprint is a mark, then what is it marking?

Not ownership. We are not possessions.

Not rank or status. The print favors no class or color, no culture or creed. It is more intimate than that. More quiet.

It marks origin.

It reminds you, "You were made." It suggests a beginning. And in doing so, it bears resemblance to something familiar in our world: a signature.

When a person signs their name to a letter, a check, a painting, a law, they are doing more than marking. They are claiming. They are saying, "This bears my intent. My design. My approval. My presence."

Could it be that the fingerprint is just that? A quiet, physical way of saying: Made by Thy.

When I scan fingerprints, they come to life under the soft light of the machine. Some spiral, others arch, others loop.

Some are deep and defined. Others are faint, fine, almost hesitant. No two are the same. But every single one is deliberate.

Over time, I noticed the patterns, though different, speak the same language. Like dialects of one origin. Like accents from a single root tongue. In a world that rushes to label us by our job, our title, our race, our politics, this print doesn't ask to be noticed. It simply exists. A truth beneath the noise.

You don't need to believe in any specific religion to feel this. You don't need to be spiritual to observe design. You only need to look. Closely. Openly. A fingerprint is not written. It is formed. Not imposed. Grown. Like the curl of a leaf. The grain of a tree. The IRIS of an eye. But unlike these, the print is ours alone. Not even identical twins share the same one.

There is no other part of the human body quite like it, unique, enduring, and quietly revealing. So, if this is a signature... what is it signing? A work of art? A living soul? A vessel of intention?

That is not for me to answer. I can only observe what I have seen: That each fingerprint, like each life, is not an accident. It is a signature. And the Maker is not silent.

Chapter 14

Designed, Not Necessary

There is a great difference between what is functional... and what is intentional.

The human body is a marvel of utility. lungs to breathe, muscles to move, a heart to pump, a brain to think. Evolutionary biologists will tell you that our bodies are shaped by what was needed to survive. If something didn't serve a survival purpose, it likely didn't endure.

But fingerprints, as miraculous as they are, are not necessary for survival.

A person without fingers can live. A person without prints can function. We have seen cases of extreme burns or rare conditions, like adermatoglyphia, the medical term for being born without fingerprints. And what do we know? Life continues. Breath continues. Existence does not require the fingerprint.

Which raises the question: If the fingerprint is not biologically essential, then why does every single human being have one?

And not just any print, but one that is impossibly unique,

intricately complex, unchanging from birth to death?

Why would nature go that far?

To create difference for the sake of difference? To add flair to the fingertips of 8 billion people for no functional reason? No. Nature does not usually work that way. Nature is efficient. Practical. Harsh, even. It does not waste energy crafting decorative designs on the surface of the skin, unless those designs mean something.

Which leads us to a different conclusion:

The fingerprint is not merely a survival tool. It is a signal. A deliberate choice in the design of the human being. An indicator that we were not just shaped, we were intended.

Even the pattern itself, loops, whorls, arches, cannot be predicted by genes alone. Two identical twins, with the same DNA, growing side by side in the same womb, will exit with entirely different fingerprints.

We cannot explain that away with "randomness." We cannot dismiss that as a coincidence.

Because coincidence may account for one or two cases.

But not every human in every time, across every culture, without any repeat.

What you carry on your fingertips is not an evolutionary byproduct.

It is a personal signature of intent.

A signature from a Mind that chooses to leave its mark, not only on mountains or oceans or stars, but on you.

You see, there are two ways to look at the fingerprint:

As a function of friction to help you grip objects (as some scientists have proposed).

As a personal mark from the Creator (as I am proposing), meant to distinguish you from every other soul that has ever lived.

You be the judge.

Which one feels more honest?

More complete?

More aligned with what your spirit already knows?

In our pursuit of logic, we have sometimes forgotten to pause in wonder. We have tried to explain the universe without acknowledging the possibility that some things were placed not to help us survive, but to remind us we were created.

Fingerprints fall into this category.

They are designed, not necessary.

They are intended, not accidental.

They are a subtle declaration from the One who made you:

"You are mine. You are different. And you were not made to be lost in the crowd."

Every time you look at your hand, that message remains quiet, unchanging, and true.

Chapter 15
The Question of Proof

It is only natural to ask: Is any of this proof?

Not suggestion. Not possibility. Not poetry.

But proof.

It is a fair question, especially in a world that honors evidence, precision, and repeatability. In science, proof must be observable. In court, proof must be admissible. In life, we often want proof to be irrefutable.

And yet, the deepest truths we carry are rarely so.

Love cannot be measured, yet it moves us.

Beauty cannot be quantified, yet we know it when we see it.

And purpose?

It evades every lab instrument ever built, yet many will cross oceans in search of it.

So, when I say that the fingerprint is the proof in the flesh, I do not claim to offer laboratory certainty. I am not holding a mathematical equation for the divine. What I am offering is something that, for many, may be more powerful: a living observation.

For more than 15 years, I have witnessed fingerprints, thousands of them, up close, one by one. I have seen children, elders, immigrants, CEOs, students, ex-convicts, mothers, veterans, citizens, skeptics, believers, strangers from every walk of life.

They spoke different languages. Wore different clothes. Carried different pasts. But when they placed their finger on that scanner, they all did the same thing: they offered something only they had. Something no one else in history, past or future, would ever duplicate.

That, to me, is data.

Not the kind you can graph or publish. But the kind you can witness.

Is that enough to prove a Creator?

Maybe not for some. But for me, it proves this:

There is a design here. And design implies a designer.

We do not create unique fingerprints for ourselves. We cannot alter them into new patterns. We can mask them, scar them, even erase them from the surface, but not from their origin. Their memory lives deep in the dermis, ready to grow again.

So if this phenomenon exists, if every human has a distinct mark that predates their thoughts, choices, or beliefs, should we not pause and ask:

Who made this possible?

Even if the answer is not God as traditionally known, it is still an answer. It is still a clue that something more than randomness is at work. That something intended us to be distinguishable.

I am not here to convince anyone. I am not preaching doctrine. I am simply saying what I have seen: a quiet miracle, repeated billions of times, and yet never the same twice. And if that is not worth calling a kind of proof, what is?

Ten Prints, One Purpose.

Ask me something else.

Are the foot prints the same as the hand prints?

No. The footprints are not the same as the handprints or fingerprints, but they share some fascinating similarities.

Here is the truth, in all its mystery:

Footprints do have ridges, much like fingerprints. The soles of the feet contain friction ridges, especially in infants, whose footprints are sometimes taken at birth for identification.

But unlike fingerprints, the patterns on the soles are not as detailed, permanent, or forensically reliable as those on the fingers. They are unique, yes, but not as complex nor as consistently used for identity verification. We don't build global biometric systems on footprints. We build them on fingerprints.

The hands, specifically the fingertips, are where the mark of the Maker is most intentionally and universally placed.

Why?

Because hands reach, touch, create, sign, bless, build, destroy, and heal.

Feet walk, carry, move, and stand, but they are not the universal tool of expression, intention, or declaration.

The fingerprint is intimate. It is how we open what is locked. How we affirm identity. How we say "Yes, it is me." The footprint is distant. It marks where we have been, not who we are.

In writing this book, I am not tracing where humanity walked.

I am attempting to explore Who touched them first. And that touch, is found on the fingertips.

Chapter 16

Each Finger Speaks a Purpose

Hold out your hands.

What you see are not just tools for labor or gestures. What you see is a living signature, divided across ten vessels, each inscribed with a mark that no one else in history has ever worn. And even more wondrous: none of your ten fingers match each other.

Not your right index and left index. Not your thumbs. Not your pinkies.

Each fingerprint is uniquely formed, uniquely yours, and uniquely different even within your own body.

Why?

Why wouldn't the Creator, who could have easily made one design and stamped it across all ten fingers, choose instead to give each its own blueprint?

Science will say it's due to random fetal pressure, or unpredictable environmental shifts in the womb. But if

randomness was truly the master, we would expect chaos, not this remarkable order through variation.

So we ask again: Why this much difference, within a single human being?

Because difference alone is not the message.

Difference in harmony, that is the divine fingerprint.

Each finger is distinct, yes. But each also contributes to a shared purpose. Together, they grasp, they hold, they build, they express, they reach. And while the prints differ, the mission unites.

The thumb is strongest, the anchor.

The index guides, the leader.

The middle finger steadies, the spine.

The ring finger symbolizes covenant, the keeper of promise.

The pinky finishes, subtle, precise.

Each one does its part. And none are repeated. Yet all were made by the same hand... for one human being.

This is where the mark of The Maker reveals itself most clearly: He does not repeat Himself, yet He does not contradict Himself.

Every finger unique. Every fingerprint different. And yet, no confusion, no conflict.

This is not a random accident of biology. This is deliberate difference within unified design. And that is what makes the human being so special:

We are not stamped once. We are signed ten times, and yet still remain one.

You are not a chaotic collection of parts.

You are a symphony of specificity.

The same Divine Author who made galaxies without duplication, made you without redundancy. The fingers don't argue. They don't fight over who matters most. Each has a role. Each has a mark. And all of them belong to you.

This is the secret your hand has been trying to tell you:

"I was made, not just once, but ten times over.

And still, I am one being. Still, I am whole."

The fingerprint does not shout the Maker's name.

It whispers it.

Repeatedly.

In every finger.

Through every touch.

In a language only the soul understands.

This page intentionally left blank for your reading reflection

Chapter 17

Our Fingerprint Has Memory

The human body forgets many things.

A scratch fades.

A bruise disappears.

A scar, over time, softens and blends.

But the fingerprint, that delicate swirl of ridges, valleys, and impressions, remembers.

Even when scraped off. Even when burned.

Even when erased, purposefully or not, it returns.

Not always perfectly, not always visibly.

But the deeper truth beneath the skin reasserts itself.

Because a fingerprint is not on the surface alone. It is formed from within.

Dermatoglyphics, the study of the patterns etched into our fingers, palms, and soles. Scientists will tell you that these prints are formed in the womb, around the 10th to 15th week of gestation.

Influenced by genetics, yes, but also by chance movements, pressures, and the unique environmental dance inside the womb. No two journeys are the same, and so no two fingerprints ever are.

And once formed, they stay the same forever.

Even when the outer skin is injured, the dermal layer below preserves the original design. And in time, when healing begins, the pattern returns, almost like the body remembering who it is. Or what it is. Or what it was made to be.

How can skin carry memory?

How can cells know what to become again?

Science has answers. But even those answers, when pressed to their core, circle back to mystery. We know the how, but the why lingers, unanswered. Or maybe better said, unclaimed.

What we do know is this:

The fingerprint is stubborn.

It resists change.

It insists on you.

In that, there is a kind of faith, not the kind taught in books or sermons, but the quiet faith of the body in itself. A loyalty to its own design.

You could call it nature. Or biology. Or intelligence. I call it a Divine signature with memory.

Because if something is written in flesh so deeply that even time, injury, and intention cannot erase it... that is not just biology.

That is belonging.

To yourself.

To a design.

To a Maker, perhaps.

The flesh remembers what the mind may forget.

In our doubt, in our despair, in our wandering, in our pain, there is still a mark. Silent. Steady. Enduring.

What kind of artist signs their work in a place so hidden, only the one who bears it can truly see?

One who didn't care for credit. Only connection.

This page intentionally left blank for your reading reflection

Chapter 18

When Identity Fails, the Fingerprint Remains

Names can change. Faces can age. Accents can be faked.

Histories can be erased. But the fingerprint... remains.

In a world obsessed with identity, we often build our sense of self on fragile foundations. Our jobs, our status, our appearance, our affiliations, all become badges of who we think we are. But remove them, and we tremble. Because deep down, we know: those things are borrowed. Temporary. Not truly ours.

But there's one part of you that has never changed, never been borrowed, never been given to anyone else.

Your fingerprint. You were born with it. You will die with it. And no one, no matter how powerful, can take it from you.

In my years observing the fingerprints of thousands of individuals, I witnessed something profound. Many came in happy, confused, broken, or uncertain about who they were. People fleeing old lives, building new ones, lost in their own past or disconnected from their own narrative.

And yet, when the finger touched the scanner, silence.

Then clarity.

That swirling, looping pattern lit up on the screen like a signature from a higher court. It didn't ask who you were pretending to be. It didn't care what you had lost, or what you were hiding.

It simply stated the truth:

> This is who you are.
>
> This is who you've always been.
>
> This is who Thy made.

In moments of personal crisis, when people forget who they are, the fingerprint remembers.

In moments of betrayal, where your name is dragged through doubt, the fingerprint remains honest.

In systems of law, when everything else can be forged, the fingerprint stands alone, immune to imitation.

We try to build our identity from the outside in. But the fingerprint reminds us: real identity is stamped from the inside out, shaped before memory, before speech, before our own awareness. Even in the most advanced biometric systems, when facial recognition fails due to lighting or angle, when voices can't be heard, when documents are questioned, the final word often comes from one place:

The finger.

Because nothing is more you… than that.

And in this, there's a whisper of divine mercy.

Even if you lose everything, your money, your title, your passport, your voice, you have not lost the most essential proof that you exist, and that you were made by design. You are still known. Still counted. Still real.

Your Maker gave you a mark that does not fade with shame, doesn't change with age, and cannot be stolen. Not even by you.

There's something almost sacred about that.

Something so deeply compassionate that, even when you forget yourself, our Creator does not.

This page intentionally left blank for your reading reflection

---

Chapter 19

The First Impression Is Lasting

Long before you spoke, before you cried, before you opened your eyes, you touched something.

Maybe it was the soft inner wall of your mother's womb. Maybe it was the air of a sterile room. Maybe it was another human hand, gloved or bare, receiving you.

And in that moment, without knowing it, you left your first impression.

Not metaphorically. Not symbolically.

You left a literal print, your fingerprint, on the world.

It may have been wiped away in seconds, but that isn't the point. The point is: you arrived with something to leave behind.

Not learned. Not earned. Not chosen.

Given.

Your fingerprint was there before your name, before your thoughts, before your memories. It was already formed, already designed, as if your body whispered to the world, "I was here. And I am me."

There is something tender about that. And something powerful. Because what else in life comes so early and stays so long?

Names can be changed. Faces can age. Voices can fade.

But the fingerprint, it stays.

It is the one truth you carry from your first moment to your last, no matter where you walk, stumble, or rise in between.

Think about this: before you ever made a choice, you had already been chosen, to bear a mark like no other.

We don't remember our first breath.

We don't recall the hand that held us first.

But our print remembers. Our body remembers.

And in that remembrance lies something humbling.

The world didn't wait for us to become significant.

It didn't wait for us to earn importance.

It stamped us, from the very beginning, with distinction.

It's easy to forget this in the noise of life.

To think our value lies in achievements, roles, or recognition.

But the fingerprint says otherwise.

It says, You were made. And you were meant.

That first impression may be invisible to the eye, but it is never erased from the story of your being. It lasts your existence.

You arrived marked, not by accident, but perhaps, by intention.

Chapter 20

The Final Proof, Touched, Signed, Sent

There comes a moment when words are no longer enough.

You can tell someone they matter. You can write books, preach sermons, paint pictures. But the deepest truths aren't spoken. They're *felt.* They're imprinted into the fabric of who we are, the kind of truth you don't need to remember because it never left you in the first place.

That's what your fingerprint is.

It's not decoration. It's not proof for science or courts alone. It's a quiet, eternal reminder that *you've already been touched.*

Not metaphorically. Not poetically.

Literally.

There, on your fingertips, is the touch that formed you. The stroke that said:

"This soul belongs to Me."

"This being is of My making."

"This one, this exact one, is needed."

And when you came into the world, you didn't carry a resume or a crown. You carried a mark.

Your fingerprint.

You arrived *touched,* you will leave *signed,* and you are now being *sent.*

Sent into life with your own unique way to hold, build, reach, give, protect, comfort, and bless.

You don't need to be famous to matter.

You don't need to be perfect to be marked.

You only need to *exist,* and you already carry the proof.

I have met thousands of people through the simple act of fingerprinting. Many were anxious, some indifferent. But occasionally, someone would pause. They'd stare at their own pattern on the screen, squinting, surprised. "Is that really mine?" they'd ask. I would nod. Every time.

And sometimes, just sometimes, they'd whisper...

"That's wild."

"That's beautiful."

"That's... something."

They were right. It *is* something. It's the final proof.

Not because it wins an argument.

Not because it converts skeptics.

But because it exists, day after day, without ever changing, without ever lying, without ever trying to prove itself.

It just *is*.

Like the One who made it.

So next time you wonder if your life matters, if you are seen, if anything about you was ever intentional...

Look at your hand.

You were touched.

And yes, *you* were signed.

Chapter 21

The Signature We Never Asked For

There are signatures we write, and then there's the one written on us.

We sign our names at the bank, the courthouse, the school, the ballot box. Each one an act of agreement, a moment of will. But even before we could hold a pen or understand a promise, a signature was already pressed into our body, not by our own hand, but into our hand.

Our fingerprint.

We didn't ask for it.

We didn't design it.

We didn't consent to it.

And yet... it is ours. Singular. Binding. Identifying.

We live in an age obsessed with autonomy, with the right to define ourselves, to choose, to declare, to redesign. And yet, the one imprint that stays with us from birth to death, the one that cannot be altered, forged, or replicated, was never chosen at all.

It was given.

Call it biology. Call it chance.

Call it divine.

Whatever name we give it, the truth remains: it precedes us. It claims us. And it cannot be undone.

What kind of mark is this, that needs no ink, no witness, no notarization, and still stands as the most reliable proof of who we are?

We try to prove ourselves in all kinds of ways. Through achievement. Through possessions. Through voice, reputation, appearance, affiliations.

But a fingerprint proves something different.

Not what we've done, but that we are.

That we exist. That we are distinct. That we are not a repeat.

It is a signature with no flourish, no ego, no noise.

And yes, no two are the same.

That kind of precision, over billions of beings, is not just impressive. It borders on impossible, unless, of course, it was meant.

There's something unsettling about that. And something comforting, too.

Because if we were marked before memory, if we were

signed before story, then maybe... just maybe... we were seen before success.

Maybe our worth does not come from effort, but from origin.

The fingerprint asks no questions. It offers no judgment.

It simply announces: This is you. And only you.

And in a world that constantly demands proof, of competence, of value, of worthiness, the fingerprint quietly provides it.

Not as a performance. But as a presence.

This page intentionally left blank for your reading reflection

_____

_____

_____

_____

_____

_____

_____

_____

_____

_____

_____

Chapter 22

The Hand of the Maker

If every human fingerprint is unique, and if no machine has ever been able to design such distinct patterns at scale, then one must ask, who did?

The answer doesn't need to be shouted, only asked.

Not from the pulpit, but from the palm.

Look at your hand.

Its creases form valleys like dried rivers.

Its ridges rise in intricate, swirling designs.

Its curves spiral in logic too subtle to trace.

This is not randomness.

It is not disorder.

It is complexity with purpose.

When we walk into a museum and gaze upon a painting of impossible detail, we never ask, did this make itself?

When we hear a symphony, layered in structure and surprise, we don't wonder if the notes accidentally arranged themselves.

We look for the artist.

We credit the composer.

And yet, the fingerprint, more intricate than brushstrokes, more deliberate than sound, has often been explained away as nature's utility. A grip aid. A skin texture. A minor evolutionary event.

But what if it's more than that?

What if it is not merely part of us, but a message to us?

Not a statement in words, but in impression.

Not loud, but lasting.

A whisper, from hand to hand, saying:

"I was here. And so are you."

The Maker, whatever name you give Him or Her or It, may not have left a signature in the sky. But perhaps, in humility, They left it somewhere smaller.

In the tip of every finger.

Where it cannot be erased.

Where it touches the world every day.

What artist signs the inside of the canvas?

What sculptor engraves the unseen edge?

A humble one. A quiet one. A certain one.

A Maker who says not "Look at Me," but "Look at you."

And that's the essence of it, isn't it?

The fingerprint does not point upward. It does not evangelize.

It points outward, into life, into others, into the world.

Every time you touch something, you leave a trace of this mark.

Every doorknob. Every page.

Every child's cheek.

Every cracked screen.

You are not just present. You are marking.

Not because you're powerful, but because you were made that way.

And maybe the proof of the Maker is not in the heavens, but in the flesh.

This page intentionally left blank for your reading reflection

_____

_____

_____

_____

_____

_____

_____

_____

_____

_____

_____

Chapter 23

When the Finger Touches the World

We don't often think of our fingerprints when we live. We teach. We eat. We reach. We type. We hold. We press.

And yet, with every action, we leave something behind.

A smudge on a glass.

A trace on a surface.

A residue of presence.

Some are visible, some vanish in seconds.

Some are never seen, yet they linger.

Some tell stories in forensic labs. Others stay forever on the skin of those we love.

The truth is simple: our fingers touch more than things, they touch lives.

We do not just leave marks on doors and surfaces and books.

We leave them on people.

On hearts. On memories. On moments.

One kind word pressed into someone's pain.

One gesture held longer than expected.

One caress on a child's forehead.

One hand extended when someone else turned away.

These, too, are fingerprints.

And they last longer than any forensic evidence.

If we were made with unique prints, then maybe we were made to leave a unique impact.

Not only in what we do, but in how we do it.

Not only in what we build, but in who we touch.

Touch, after all, is the first language we speak.

It comforts before words.

It reassures beyond logic.

It remembers what the mind forgets.

When your finger touches the world, you do more than interact, you declare:

I am here. I am part of this moment. And it will not be the same without me.

But this is not about ego. It's about responsibility.

Because if we are always leaving something behind, then we must choose what we leave.

Do we leave bruises or blessings?

Do we smudge or shape?

Do we trace harm or healing?

Each day gives us countless chances to decide.

You can touch with force, or you can touch with grace.

You can grasp, or you can give.

You can press down, or you can lift up.

And though no one may see the print, the world feels it.

People carry it.

Sometimes forever.

So when your finger touches the world, pause.

And ask: What do I want to leave here?

Because you will leave something.

Even silence has its mark.

Even absence makes an impression.

In the end, your fingerprint is not just a pattern. It is a possibility.

A quiet invitation to touch this world with the same care, intention, and wonder with which you were made.

Chapter 24

When the Finger Is Gone

What happens when the finger is no longer there to touch the world?

When the hand rests still.

When the ridges no longer press into paper, glass, skin, or soil.

When breath has stopped, and flesh returns to dust.

Does the fingerprint vanish?

Yes, physically, it does. The skin softens. The lines fade.

Eventually, the body itself becomes memory.

But the mark is another matter.

Because fingerprints are not limited to the skin. Some are left in places no microscope can find.

They're pressed into the minds of children.

Embedded in the trust of those we once held. Etched into letters written long ago.

Carried in the way someone says our name, even when we are gone.

Our fingerprints, those quiet proofs of uniqueness, outlive our hands.

They echo.

In behaviors we shaped. In love we gave.

In harm we may regret. In grace we extended without knowing it would be our last chance.

We worry, sometimes, about our legacy, as if it's something we must construct or broadcast. But perhaps legacy is something much simpler. Much quieter.

It is what we touched, and how we touched it.

The table we built.

The face we wiped.

The hurt we eased.

The apology we made.

The hands we held in their most vulnerable moments.

These things linger long after the finger is gone.

And here's the haunting beauty: even those who tried to erase themselves, those who felt invisible, unseen, unworthy, even they left fingerprints.

Even they touched the world in ways they may never know. Perhaps that's why this print matters so much.

Because it's not just evidence of who we were.

It's a symbol that we were.

That we didn't pass through this life untouched or untouched by it.

That something, someone, marked us into being.

And that in return, we were meant to mark something back.

So yes, the finger goes.

But the fingerprint, in every sense of the word, remains.

It remains in stories told at kitchen tables.

In photos held gently by the aging.

In the instinct of a daughter's laugh.

In the silence of a room that still holds our presence.

And if all we were is gone, yet something of us stays, maybe that is the point.

Maybe this was never about immortality, but about intimacy. Not about living forever but about having lived.

When the finger is gone, the question becomes:

What did I touch, and how did I touch it?

Let that be your legacy. Let that be your fingerprint.

Chapter 25

The Invisible Ink

There's something unique about our fingerprints.

They are physical, traceable, undeniable, and yet, most of the time, they are invisible.

You press your finger to a surface, and unless dust or ink betrays you, nothing appears.

No mark, no stain, no proof. And yet forensics will tell you, the print is there.

Invisible to the eye.

Real to the trained. Permanent to the record.

We live much of life like this.

Most of our impact isn't visible in the moment. No applause. No headlines. No evidence of our kindness, our restraint, our effort.

You can give someone the truth they didn't want to hear with compassion.

You can stay when others would've walked away.

You can choose to love quietly, and no one may notice.

But the ink is there.

Invisible. And still recording.

It's in the way someone feels safer around you without knowing why.

In the way a stranger breathes easier after your brief presence.

In the tone your children carry into their own parenting.

In the courage you gave someone simply by listening, and believing them.

We often ask, "What difference did I make?"

And if we don't see one, we fear the answer is "None." But not all difference is seen.

There's ink beneath the surface.

And sometimes, it only reveals itself much later, when a life suddenly blooms because of something planted long ago. A word. A gesture. A touch. A moment.

In this way, the fingerprint becomes metaphor.

A reminder that what matters most is not always measured.

That the evidence of your being is not only in what you do, but in the unseen ways you shaped the world around you.

It's how light travels, even after the star has died.

And so, when you doubt your presence, when the world seems to forget what you've given, remember:

You're writing in invisible ink.

But it's still being read.

Not by everyone.

Not always by those you hoped. But by someone. Somewhere. Someone who needed it. Someone who may never say it aloud. Someone who may never even know it was you, only that something shifted in them after your touch, your word, your grace.

And perhaps that is the quietest proof of all: that you were not made merely to be seen, but to be felt.

To walk this world as a living fingerprint, leaving traces of compassion, of dignity, of intention, even when no one is watching. Especially then.

This page intentionally left blank for your reading reflection

_____

_____

_____

_____

_____

_____

_____

_____

_____

_____

_____

Chapter 26

The Twin That Never Was

Science tells us something that should stop us in our tracks: Even identical twins, who share the same DNA, do not share the same fingerprints.

Let that settle in.

Two people, born of the same genetic code, growing in the same womb, fed by the same blood, at the same time, yet they emerge with fingerprints that do not match.

Why?

Scientists give several reasons:

Minor differences in pressure.

Slight shifts in amniotic fluid.

Random micro-movements in the womb.

They say fingerprints are shaped not just by DNA, but by the environment, by touch, by tension, by chance.

But what if it's not just that? What if this is one more our

Maker's gentle whisper?

A gentle insistence that even if everything else about you resembles another, your fingerprint will still say:

Not quite.

This one is mine.

Made not by mere biology, but by decision.

Maybe not yours. But someone's.

The twin that never was, because even in sameness, we were not meant to be copies.

We were meant to be distinct.

Carved with just enough difference to bear our own story.

To hold our own mirror.

To leave our own mark.

This is not to deny our common humanity.

We bleed alike. We break alike. We heal alike.

But the fingerprint reminds us that sameness is not the goal. Uniqueness is. Even if you walk beside someone.

Chapter 27

The Reflection of the Maker

Look again.

Not at the sky.

Not at the stars.

Not at the oceans, the mountains, or the galaxies we so often name as the evidence of wonder.

Look at your own hand.

There it is, soft or calloused, smooth or worn, trembling or steady. It does not matter. Because in its center, pressed into every finger, is a design no one else has. Not in your city. Not in your family. Not in the history of humankind.

That is the signature.

Not of a machine. Not of mutation. Not of mindless accident. But of a Designer.

One who gently whispered, this one… this one I will make unlike any other.

This book has not sought to prove God with charts or sermons. It has not begged belief. It has only invited noticing.

Noticing the ridges.

Noticing the patterns.

Noticing that the same precision seen in galaxies is pressed into your fingertips.

The same order. The same quiet intelligence.

The same mystery.

Your fingerprint is not divine. But it points.

It hints. It tells a silent truth:

That whoever made you, did not make you carelessly.

You were meant. Not in grandeur. But in detail. And the detail is enough.

The fingerprint, in its quiet spiral, is not a claim of faith. It is an invitation to awe.

Not to believe blindly, but to wonder courageously.

To say:

If this is in me, what else might be?

And if I was made, what was I made for?

The proof is not on the wall.

It is in the flesh.

Not just to see yourself, but to glimpse the possibility that you were not only born, you were crafted.

Made by what?

By Whom?

That is not mine to answer.

But I do know this: Your fingerprint holds the question. And perhaps, that is more powerful than any answer ever written.

This page intentionally left blank for your reading reflection

Chapter 28
When Data Points to Design

As a graduate of MIT's advanced program in Machine Learning and Data Science, through Great Learning, I have spent a great time immersed in models, algorithms, and pattern recognition. These tools sharpen our ability to measure, predict, and optimize. But there is a deeper question that data alone doesn't answer: what if what we are measuring is already evidence of a higher order?

In thousands of fingerprint scans across gender, race, age, and background, the data was clear: not one print was identical to another. If randomness were the only driver, occasional duplication would occur. In every scan, I observed complete uniqueness. This isn't just anomaly, it's consistency in individuality. And that is where data begins to present a definitive design.

In data science, we prize outliers, patterns, and uniform distribution. But here, the pattern is the lack of pattern, the system itself refuses repetition. Such complexity, delivered universally and consistently, begs the question:

what algorithm, what code, what force ensures this uniqueness at birth, in every human?

We can model the ridges, scan the minutiae points, store them in massive databases. We can even simulate fingerprint generation with artificial neural networks. But we still cannot create a human fingerprint from scratch with the same organic intricacy and irreproducibility. That limitation humbles science and opens the door to awe.

So this book is not an argument against science and found data. It is a plea to listen to what the data might be telling us.

That perhaps, behind every print, there is a Printer.

That perhaps, behind every design, there is a Designer.

That perhaps, behind every creation, there is a Creator.

That every identity logged in a system is also etched by a Signature not yet quantifiable.

We may never write the equation for "Made by Thy." But sometimes, what we cannot model… is the clearest model of all.

Chapter 29
Made by Thy

I did not see it at first. Initially, I saw the swirls, the loops, the ridges, the whorls pressed into fingertip after fingertip, on form after form, across race, age, gender, creed.

I saw the beauty of biology. The logic of pattern. The strangeness of difference.

I had touched the prints of thousands. Printed thousands more. And somewhere along the way, the seeing changed.

It wasn't just that the prints were unique. It was that they were consistent in their uniqueness.

Each one is different, Each one was made with intention. Like brushstrokes by the same invisible hand, none repeated, none random, none wrong.

And a thought came.

If this is not art, what is?

If this is not design, then why does it feel like a signature, a unique mark?

Made by whom?

The question echoed through years of quiet observation.

It wasn't answered by religion. Nor by rebellion.

Nor even by reason.

It was answered by the fingerprint itself.

Not loudly. Not in proof. But in presence.

There is a kind of proof that doesn't argue.

It simply is. A soft reminder in the flesh that says, I was made.

And then, deeper still:

I was made... by Someone.

Not by "what."

By Thy.

The word we reach for when words fail. The Name without spelling. The Voice without voice. The Maker behind the mark.

Call it God.

Call it Creator.

Call it What Moves All.

This is not a doctrine. This is a surrender.

Because at some point, we stop asking How was I made? and begin asking Why?

That's when the print becomes a path.

A starting point, an opening into the unknown, yet present. And that is why this book is titled what it is.

Made by Thy.

Not as a conclusion. Not as certainty. But as reverence.

Not to persuade. But to honor the quiet truth beneath the skin:

You are not just here. You were placed.

You were formed.

You were... made by Thy.

And that, perhaps, is the most sacred knowing of all.

This page intentionally left blank for your reading reflection

_____

_____

_____

_____

_____

_____

_____

_____

_____

_____

Chapter 30

You Are Free to Disagree

By now, someone reading may be thinking, "This isn't proof." "This isn't science." ... "This doesn't belong in the realm of evidence."

To that, I say gently: Perhaps you're right. And possibly you're not. I'm not here claiming that fingerprints are irrefutable, scientific proof of the existence of a Maker, a Creator.

I'm not a physicist writing about quantum theology. I'm not a theologian constructing doctrine.

I am a man, a professional scholar, as part of his family business, in the last 15 years, I have fingerprinted thousands of people. I have seen the prints with my own eyes. I have placed their fingers on the flat glass of our DOJ and FBI certified scanner. I have watched the pattern appear on the screen, unique and different every time.

And over time, that left an impression on me. A scholarly observation of sort. Not just from what I saw, but from what it meant.

Fingerprints are real. Their uniqueness is real. Their consistency is real.

Their permanence is real. But what they point to, what they suggest, that's where meaning comes in. That's where interpretation begins. That's where the line between observation and belief is crossed.

I crossed it.

Not because I needed to. But because after thousands of fingerprints, I couldn't deny what I was witnessing anymore. Patterns that never repeat.

Designs that serve no evolutionary survival advantage. Variation that exists not just across people, but within each person.

Yes, I know what science says: pressure in the womb, friction, random development. I have read the journals. I respect the science. I don't argue with the biology.

But I ask: Why such beautiful randomness?

Why this much variation? Why this personal precision? And why, of all places, put it on our hands, the very part of our body that touches the world?

Science did not give me the answers.

Maybe science will never answer that. Maybe it doesn't need to. But I saw it, again and again, and I began to feel something many won't admit:

This doesn't feel accidental.

You're free to disagree. But don't ignore this:

These are the lived observations of someone who has touched thousands of human lives, not through theory, but through real fingertips pressed to real fingerprint scanner.

I didn't start this book to win a debate. I'm not here to argue. I wrote it because I have seen too much not to say something. And what I have seen, in you, in everyone, is a quiet mark that says:

You were made.

That's not English. That's not science.

That is truth, the kind only your hand can tell.

This page intentionally left blank for your reading reflection

_____

_____

_____

_____

_____

_____

_____

_____

_____

_____

_____

Chapter 31: Author's Final Notes

When we look at our hands, we rarely think about the story they have carried since the beginning of our existence. We see lines, shapes, wrinkles, and perhaps a few scars that life placed there. We rarely stop long enough to notice the one detail that belongs only to us.

Well, the most permanent truth about our identity sits openly on the surface of our skin. It has been there from the first moments of life, and it will remain there until we take our final breath.

As a humble researcher and a modest scholar, for many years I believed meaning had to come from complicated explanations. I thought it must come from study, belief, or answers that required long thinking. In researching for this book, I realized something different. Some truths are so simple that we miss them while searching for something greater. We do not need to travel far to discover who we are. Our identity has always been within reach, resting on our own fingertips.

A fingerprint does not ask to be believed. It does not need agreement or permission. It does not argue with anyone.

It simply lives, quietly, without interruption, and it continues after we depart. Even in moments of doubt, the fingerprint remains unchanged. When we question our worth, it continues to say the same thing. When we feel invisible, it continues to exist. When we forget who we are, it still remembers.

There is a kind of dignity in that silence. There is a message written into our biology that stands without speaking. We were born with a signature, with a mark that will never repeat in the story of another human being.

We arrived with uniqueness already written into us, before we contributed anything to the world. Long before we tried to understand purpose, purpose was already present.

We spend much of our life searching for validation. We search for acceptance, recognition, belonging, and love. Yet long before anyone knew us, something formed within us that confirmed we mattered. We did not need to earn this confirmation. We did not need to deserve it. We simply received it as part of our creation.

If there is a quiet message in the fingerprint, it may be this. You are not an accident of nature. You are an expression of life that refuses to copy itself. And that alone is a form of meaning.

I do not claim to know the full intention behind this design. I do not claim to possess absolute truth. I have only observed what is already there. But every time I watched another fingerprint appear on a screen, I felt something inside me settle. I felt that existence made a decision long before I learned how to make any decisions of my own.

Perhaps the fingerprint is not meant to convince us of anything. Perhaps its purpose is simply to remind us that individuality was placed inside every human being with remarkable care. When everything else changes, when life becomes uncertain, when our path becomes difficult, we still carry a pattern that says we were known from the beginning.

So if you finish this book with only one thought, let it be this. Meaning is not something you must search for outside yourself. Meaning is already within you. Look at your fingertips. That is your beginning. That is your proof. That is your quiet signature of your Maker.

Dr. Abe.

This page intentionally left blank for your reading reflection

Interview with the Author

"Q&A"

This page intentionally left blank for your reading reflection

---

Interview with the Author

"Q&A"

Author: Dr. Abraham Khoureis, Ph.D.

Author of Made by Thy: The Proof in the Flesh
Published by Ang Power Publishing House.

Question (Q): What inspired you to write Made by Thy: The Proof in the Flesh?

Dr. Abraham's Answer (A): For over a decade, I worked with thousands of fingerprints through my background screening company. Few years back, I realized I wasn't just looking at biometric data, I was witnessing a design. Not one fingerprint was alike. The more I observed, the more I began to feel that these impressions weren't just of a human, they were by something greater. This book is my response to that quiet revelation.

Q: Is this a religious book?

A: No. And yes. It's not religious in the traditional sense, I don't preach doctrine or push belief. But it is reverent. It opens a door to something sacred that many may call God. Others may call it Nature, the Universe, or Consciousness. Whatever name one uses, this book respects the intelligence behind human existence, and invites readers to consider it anew.

Q: You say the fingerprint is "proof." What do you mean by that?

A: I don't mean legal proof or laboratory evidence. I mean the kind of proof that doesn't argue, it simply is. The fingerprint is the one thing every human has, and yet no two are the same. That kind of consistent uniqueness, to me, points to an intention: Of authorship. Of origin.

Q: What do you hope readers walk away with?

A: I hope they pause. I hope they look at their own hand and see not just skin, but a message. A sign that they were not thrown into this world but placed. Made. That realization alone can shift how we treat ourselves, others, and even life itself.

Q: Who is this book for?

A: It's for thinkers. Seekers. Observers. For anyone who has ever asked, "Why am I here?" or "Is there meaning behind my being?" It's also for readers tired of being told what to believe, who instead want to be invited to see something they may have missed.

Q: How is this book different from other works on identity or faith?

A: This book doesn't start with belief. It starts with observation, with the body. With something every human has: a fingerprint. From there, it reflects outward toward meaning. It's grounded in observation, not ideology. And it allows the reader to draw their own conclusion, which I believe is the most respectful kind of truth-telling.

Q: What does the title "Made by Thy" mean to you?

A: "Thy" is the sacred "You." The eternal Other. It's my way of referring to God without confining the word. The title is both a declaration and a surrender: I am made... and not by myself. I am made by Thy.

Q: Are you planning to speak, teach, or host events about this topic?

A: Yes. I'm open to speaking at universities, faith communities, spiritual gatherings, and anywhere curiosity is welcomed. This topic isn't exclusive; it belongs to every human. I'd love to help bring it to the surface through dialogue.

This page intentionally left blank for your reading reflection

---

References

Recommended Readings

Bommanavar, S., Anj, M., Karuppaiah, M., Ingale, Y., & Ingale, M. (2020). Dermatoglyphics: A concise review on basic embryogenesis, classification and theories of formation of fingerprints. *Journal of Forensic Dental Sciences, 12*(2), 120–126.

Glover, J. D., et al. (2023). The developmental basis of fingerprint pattern formation and variation. *Cell, 186*(3), 1–14. https://doi.org/10.1016/j.cell.2023.01.015

Kahn, H. S., et al. (2008). A fingerprint characteristic associated with early prenatal environment and volar pad regression. *American Journal of Human Biology, 20*(2), 151–158.

Kücken, M., & Newell, A. C. (2005). Fingerprint formation. *Journal of Theoretical Biology, 235*, 71–83. https://doi.org/10.1016/j.jtbi.2004.12.017

Sharma, A., et al. (2018). Dermatoglyphics: A review on fingerprints and their applications. *Journal of Child and Adolescent Health, 5*(3), 120–131.

Singh, A., Gupta, R., Zaidi, S. H. H., & Singh, A. (2016). Dermatoglyphics: A brief review. *International Journal of Advanced and Integrated Medical Sciences, 1*(3), 111–115.

Sudha, P. I., et al. (2021). The dermal ridges as the infallible signature of skin. *Dermatology and Genetics, 3*(1), 45–52.

Wertheim, K., et al. (n.d.). Embryology and morphology of friction-ridge skin. *National Institute of Justice Special Publication.*

About Dr. Abraham Khoureis, Ph.D.

Dr. Abraham Khoureis, Ph.D., was named the Apostle of Compassionate Leadership by his colleagues and leadership professional inner circle. A multi-talented thought leader and partner, author, an award-winning mentor, and advocate for compassionate leadership. He is an adjunct professor who specializes in teaching graduate-level courses in business and management, blending academic theory with real-world business practices.

Dr. Khoureis is also a successful small business owner and holds numerous state certifications and professional designations showcasing his multidisciplinary expertise.

He is the Creator and Developer of the Compassionate Leadership Model and Pyramid, which emphasizes leadership built on self-awareness, mindfulness, and commitment to serving others without expectation of return.

Moreover, Dr. Khoureis developed the Disability Learning Attainment Model, a framework designed to empower individuals with disabilities through inclusive education, skill-building, and leadership development. Through his writing, he advocates and advances positive societal change. His work champions and empowers inclusivity, accessibility, and ethical practices in both education and leadership. He has been published on *Forbes.com*, *Newsweek.com*, and the distinguished *Leader to Leader Journal*. He was recognized as LinkedIn's Top Leadership and Management Voice, and Thinkers 360's Top 50 Voices.

Dr. Abe's contributions extend to his writings, professional leadership development initiatives, and thought leadership, making him a respected emerging leader in the fields of compassionate leadership, organizational behavior, and human development.

Easily accessible at: DrAbeKhoureis.com

Social Media: @DrAbeKhoureis

DrAbeBooks.com – AuthorAbeKhoureis.com

For his latest published work, also visit Amazon.com

Search for Dr. Abraham Khoureis, Ph.D.

Other Books by Dr. Abraham

The Balance In Between: Finding the Balance Between Emotional Intelligence and Emotional Stupidity. ISBN: 979-8-9895211-2-8

Decoding Microaggressions for Leaders and Beyond: Understanding Microaggressions Face-to-Face. ISBN: 979-8-9895211-4-2

Hollywood Dream: How To Make It In Tinseltown. ISBN: 979-8-9895211-7-3

Protect Your Business: Stay Informed, Stay Ahead ISBN: 978-1-966837-09-1

Reasonable Accommodation: Empowering Inclusion. ISBN: 979-8-9895211-3-5

Revealing the Seven Secrets to Exceptional Mentorship. ISBN: 978-1-966837-00-8

SELF: Introducing The Self Rotating Model ISBN: 979-8-9895211-5-9

The Compassionate Leadership Model and Pyramid. ISBN: 979-8-9895211-0-4

www.ingramcontent.com/pod-product-compliance
Lightning Source LLC
Chambersburg PA
CBHW030020290326
41934CB00005B/423